100

THINGS TO DO IN
SAN JOSE
BEFORE YOU
DIE

100

THINGS TO DO IN SAN JOSE BEFORE YOU DIE

• •

SUSANNAH GREENWOOD

Library of Congress Control Number: 2015930934

ISBN: 9781681060033

Design by Jill Halpin

Cover Image: Evelyn Seto

Printed in the United States of America
15 16 17 18 19   5 4 3 2 1

Please note that websites, phone numbers, addresses, and company names are subject to change or cancellation. We did our best to relay the most accurate information available, but due to circumstances beyond our control, please do not hold us liable for misinformation. When exploring new destinations, please do your homework before you go.

CONTENTS

• •

• •

FOREWORD

You can't possibly tell San Jose you only want 100 of its "things." That only 100 of these things inside or nearby its precious boundaries are things you need to do before you die. That's just nonsense. San Jose won't have it. No, San Jose won't listen because there are thousands of stories and delightful discoveries all around this tenth largest city in the United States.

So I told San Jose these were just the *first* 100 things to do. San Jose started to object, not liking to be told what to do (this clearly stemming from its years of pioneering and innovation), but I made my case. These 100 things, they're just suggestions. San Jose didn't totally buy it, but the protest seemed to subside.

To explore San Jose properly, to really get in the spirit, get inside its head, you need to think like the founding visionaries. You can start with a plan, an idea, or inspiration (thus this book), but ultimately, the best way is to find your own path, a new way—your own way to San Jose.

The pages here are as much a love letter to the diverse and eclectic people that make up San Jose as they are a guide to its attractions, for you will meet amazing people while you mine these nuggets of fun and adventure. And I have to agree with San Jose on this point: you really can't fit all of them in a book.

● ●

I hope the distinct and varied rhythms I've tried to capture on these pages—the cadence of San Jose's fascinating history, exciting present, and bright future—inspire you to dance to the beat of your own drum.

ACKNOWLEDGMENTS

My sincere thanks to Team San Jose, Evelyn Seto, Reedy Press, the San Jose Downtown Association, the City of San Jose, and the people of San Jose; past, present, and future.

Mom, Dad, Sandy, Rebecca, Brette, Espe, Mark, Jason, Kayla, Westley, Alex, and Elizabeth; thanks for winning the gene pool.

Paxton and Lincoln (the 3-legged wonder cats), you probably can't read this, but just in case; thanks for your supreme patience and purrs.

To all my friends, teachers, coaches, mentors, and guardians; thanks for making this a fascinating journey, one that continues to thrill and amuse me.

Thanks must also be extended to the internet, sunny days, red wine, tacos, Elon Musk, wagging dog tails, flip-flops, dinosaurs, vanilla gelato, caffeine, my trusty Jeep, Pluto (you were robbed), Lasik eye surgery, the moment, music, the Doma-Cile, puns, Science, snarky hashtags, free parking, hats, and wanderlust.

To anyone who thinks they can't write a book, think again.

FOOD AND DRINK

TAKE ON
TACO TUESDAY

We take our tacos very, *very* seriously here. While we locals consider each day of the week equally appropriate for tacos, Tuesday is kind of the taco birthday of the week. From high end to hole in the wall, and from traditional to experimental, the taco is revered and interpreted pretty much 24/7. The only limit to the filling is your imagination. Time stops for the taco in San Jose— we even have a Taco Festival of Innovation each May. There are hundreds of places to get your taco fix, and each culture has its own take on this perfect little food.

Good for families

Authentic Traditional Fare

Caguamas Tacos y Mariscos
1289 S 1st St., San Jose, 95110
408-975-6648

Angelou's Mexican Grill
21 N 2nd St., San Jose, 95113
408-971-2287, www.angelousmexicangrill.com

Exquisite Fish Tacos
Dia de Pesca
55 N Bascom Ave., San Jose, 95128
408-287-3722, www.pescasifood.com

For the More Exotic Palate
Loteria Taco Bar
87 N San Pedro St., San Jose, 95110
408-580-6917, www.loteriatacobar.com

Zona Rosa
1411 The Alameda, San Jose, 95126
408-275-1411, www.zonarosasj.com

Taco Festival of Innovation
www.facebook.com/tacofestival

INTRODUCE YOUR TASTE BUDS

TO THE BEST CROISSANT OUTSIDE OF FRANCE AT LA LUNE SUCRÉE

Behold, the real breakfast of champions, the breakfast sandwich from La Lune Sucrée. On a paseo where the people and dog watching is first class, you'll find this tiny café run by super-friendly, European-trained pastry chefs. While their crepes and other treats made fresh daily are outstanding, the item that really takes the cake is the breakfast sandwich on a croissant. The heavenly crescent flakiness has the birds lined up on the patio waiting for the chance of a crumb. The hollandaise is creamy addiction with just the right tang. Combine that with perfectly poached eggs, melted gruyere, and a slice of ham, and you may find yourself throwing out all your cereal, your waffle maker, and jam. Breakfast will never be the same. Ever.

La Lune Sucrée, 116 Paseo de San Antonio, San Jose, 95113
408-292-2070, www.lalunesucree.com

Good for families

SAMPLE A BIT OF THE BIG EASY
AT THE POOR HOUSE BISTRO

I know you were just thinking, "Where can I park my krewe for a little down-home NOLA spice and laid-back music?" Don't be getting all mardi up in my gras; San Jose has you covered if you're craving Cajun. Slide on up to the Poor House Bistro and laissez les bon temps rouler. This converted Victorian with more outside than inside seating is a local favorite. Along with the expected traditional N'awlins faves like jambalaya, crawfish, and po'boys, the Creole Sunday brunch items, such as BBQ shrimp Benedict, will have you convinced you've been transported to the gulf. Add to that the best corn muffin on the entire planet and seven days a week of live jazz, blues, and rock, and you have your slice of Louisiana without trading in a single string of beads for it.

Poor House Bistro, 91 S Autumn St., San Jose, 95110
408-292-5837, www.poorhousebistro.com

STEEP A WHILE
AT SATORI TEA COMPANY

Part Downton Abbey, part apothecary, and part Mad Hatter, this crazy little teahouse is a hidden gem. Walking in is how I'd imagine discovering a fairy kingdom would feel. Magical, twee, cluttered, and charming, the décor is a patchwork of mismatched table settings and lace. Hovering somewhere between acceptable chaos and polite adventure, all with the help of a warm teapot muse, the distinct East meets West touches and altogether inexplicably odd bits about the walls are a feast for the imagination. You've plenty to take in while you wait for freshly made tea sandwiches, petit fours, scones, crumpets, and of course tea. A variety of scrumptious tea services are available with roughly a zillion types of tea for consumption and sale. Satori is your go-to place for tea-laced tranquility with a lump of whimsy.

Satori Tea Company, 37 N San Pedro St., San Jose, 95110
408-292-1502, www.satoriteausa.com

Good for families

SAVOR THE MOMENT
AT THE EXQUISITE LE PAPILLON

Admittedly, Le Papillon's understated outside doesn't exude five-star dining, but its presentable yet humble exteriors are forgotten the moment you walk in the door. The flavors, the plating, the service, it's all top-notch with a wine list to die for. This is fine French cuisine with plenty of international and *Top Chef*–type flair and surprisingly ample serving sizes and very reasonable prices considering its culinary bliss. Please observe: this may be the only place you will *not* find a cell phone at the table. Yes, sadly, cell phones are banned, so your food porn Instagrams will have to be replaced by actual, in-the-moment dining, and you'll have to tell your friends about the perfection of every dish using your words. Frightening at first, refreshing and totally worth it, though—once you cut the cord.

Le Papillon, 410 Saratoga Ave., San Jose, 95129
408-296-3730, www.lepapillon.com

"RAV ON"
AT BERTUCELLI'S LA VILLA DELICATESSEN

Ravioli. Done right, it's a pretty perfect little pillow of mouth happy, no? Especially when they're homemade, fresh, hot, right out of the pot, and smothered with freakishly amazing marinara. Comfort food times infinity. Ask anyone in San Jose where to get the best ravioli in town (and possibly in the universe) and with the exception of a few who'll say their Nonna, their answer is going to be La Villa. It's really a no-brainer. I mean, when one has a tab on their website dedicated *just* to ravioli orders, you know you're staring at a pretty legendary purveyor of ravioli. While the cheese ravs are delectably divine, the lobster, chicken, feta, and beef are all acclaimed too. Incidentally, there's a reason you can purchase online up to twenty boxes of forty-eight ravioli at a time—the all–La Villa ravioli, all-the-time diet; it's totally a thing here.

Bertucelli's La Villa Delicatessen, 1319 Lincoln Ave., San Jose, 95125
408-295-7851, www.wglavilla.com

Good for families

BRAVE
THE SIX-LEGGED APPETIZERS AT MEZCAL

Whether or not you need the extra liquid courage provided by Mezcal's notable collection of tequilas and mezcales in order to partake in the chapulines (fried grasshoppers sautéed with garlic, lime, and salt), the colorful restaurant serves both. If the owner, Adolfo, is there, he'll even give you a lesson on the differences between various tequilas and mescales just in case that helps work up your nerve. Then again, if shots or six-legged things aren't your bag, the many other family recipes will certainly please the palate. Oaxacan cuisine has a French influence resulting from a large immigration during the 1800s. Its unique blend of New World European and Old World indigenous flavors really sets it apart as a special dining experience (with or without an insect course). With three types of homemade moles, fresh guacamole made for you tableside, and Mexican desserts, there's no possibility you'll leave hungry or unhappy.

Mezcal, 25 W San Fernando St., San Jose, 95113
408-283-9595, www.mezcalrestaurantsj.com

TAME THE HUNGER BEAST
AT MOVEABLE FEAST

Food trucks. Maybe you have heard of them? The weekly assemblies of food trucks in San Jose (part of Moveable Feast) are a phenomenon many thought would be a short-lived fad and years later have proven the skeptics completely wrong. The perfect option for the indecisive, big-appetited family, coworkers with differentiating tastes, and the adventurous diner, these grub-slinging gatherings bring pretty much all the kinds of foods there are to one convenient location. This may not actually ease the decision making in the overall scheme of things, but you won't lack for affordable, quick, dish-cleaning-free options for sustenance. It's also a great place to meet people, discover new food, and catch a few hours of those famous three hundred days of sunshine.

Moveable Feast, www.mvblfeast.com

Monday dinner, 525 Blossom Hill Rd., San Jose, 95123

Wednesday dinner, 310 Crescent Village Cir., San Jose, 95134

Friday dinner, 2310 Canoas Garden Ave., San Jose, 95125

Good for families

FALL IN LINE
AT FALAFEL'S DRIVE-IN

When a restaurant is new, you can count on a certain amount of temporary, line-forming fanaticism. It's harder to write off a line after the first year or so of operation. What you cannot ignore is the line that has formed outside Falafel's Drive-In since it opened in 1966. I know. There's a lot going on with that name. It's a bit of a mystery. But wait, there's more. Besides homemade falafel and a variety of Middle Eastern menu items, what makes this place even more of an enigma is that you can get burgers and fries and even corn dogs here, too. The falafel is quite good, but let's shoot straight: there's something about a place called Falafel's Drive-In and fifty years of lining up that just has to be experienced.

Falafel's Drive-In, 2301 Stevens Creek Blvd., San Jose, 95128
408-294-7886, www.falafelsdrivein.com

Good for families

LIVE THE SWEET LIFE
AT PETER'S BAKERY

Since 1936 sweet teeth have been traveling miles to Peter's Bakery to partake of the magical baked goods that are created fresh, on-site each morning. This small, friendly bakery in Little Portugal was founded on hard work and a passion for carefully crafting desserts. Known especially for their burnt almond cake, which impresses even the most discerning taste buds, their authentic Portuguese sweet breads, éclairs, custards, and strawberry rings are also highly coveted. As the oldest family-run bakery in Silicon Valley, Peter's is nothing short of a San Jose institution. And in addition to lining the masses up in front of their own store, the impact of this historic business reaches far and wide by way of the hundreds of bakers who were trained by founder Tony Peters.

Peter's Bakery, 3108 Alum Rock Ave., San Jose, 95127, 408-258-3529

TIP
Peter's Bakery is closed on Sundays and is cash only, so for optimal enjoyment make sure you arrive with plenty of the green stuff in addition to an empty stomach.

BELIEVE THE HYPE
AT WHOLE FOODS ON THE ALAMEDA

Okay, I know what you are thinking. Why is a healthy grocery store ranked in the top one hundred? In true San Jose style, we didn't just open a Whole Foods, oh no, we put a rooftop brewery and bar on it. And then we added pop-up shopping, free bike clinics, local art, and shop for local charity days to the mix. This is a place that had all of San Jose lined up around the block for the grand opening. But seriously, it's kind of epic. Okay, it might seem like a cult, but you have to admit, even if it were, it's a pretty awesome one. You have to see it to believe it.

Whole Foods, 777 The Alameda, San Jose, 95126
408-207-1126, www.wholefoodsmarket.com

TAKE YOUR SWEET OLD TIMEY
AT ORCHESTRIA PALME COURT

It must be the healthful ingredients in reasonable portions that set Orchestria Palme Court apart from other restaurants. Of course, it could be that their old-fashioned soda fountain has something to do with it. Then again, it might be their no-rush, no-table-wait-staff, stay-all-night-if-you-want approach to dining that's really brining in the crowds. No, wait, I wonder if the fact that they match their restaurant's musical focus to the local arts events going on around them has anything to do with their popularity. It might just be that within the rustic walls of the restored 1910 building there are over a dozen vintage player pianos, orchestrions, and jukeboxes, providing unparalleled old-timey ambiance. I know, it's all of the above.

Orchestria Palme Court, 27 E Williams St., San Jose, 95112
408-288-5606, www.orchestriapalmcourt.com

TIP
With its special concept comes even more special hours, so make sure to check whether they are open before you swing by.

GET SHAKEN AND STIRRED
AT THE FAIRMONT LOBBY LOUNGE

A menu with five hundred different martinis. This should pretty much sell the Fairmont Lobby Lounge experience in and of itself, don't you think? Five hundred. That's not a typo. Yes, this is a beautiful lounge. Yes, it's open late. Yes, this is a fine place to dance to live bands, watch sports, canoodle, or relax by live piano. But more important, there exists a menu of five hundred martinis. That's just martinis. The magical menu includes seventy pages of cocktails you can order. And here's the genius part: just in case you try to order all five hundred, the Fairmont San Jose also happens to be a hotel with over eight hundred rooms available for sleeping in. Many of them provide stunning views of the city, so you can always just stay the night. Five hundred, people! That's martini madness!

Fairmont Lobby Lounge, 170 S Market St., San Jose, 95113
408-998-1900, www.fairmont.com/san-jose/dining/

DEVOUR
AWARD-WINNING POKE
AT DA KINE ISLAND GRILL

There are certainly days when sipping a tropical drink out of a pineapple and dining on award-winning ahi poke just seems like it's the answer to everything. I'm going to let you in on a secret. Sometimes it is, and Da Kine can hook you up. For your fabulous fruit fix, order the mai tai or the piña colada, which are indeed served inside a pineapple. Both the ahi and salmon poke are out of this world, but the extensive menu of authentic island dishes, like loco moco, Spam musubi, and kalua pork sliders, certainly makes you want to extend your culinary vacation. You can't help but go all macadamia nuts for this place.

Da Kine Island Grill, 23 N Market St., San Jose, 95113
408-713-2900, www.dakineislandgrill.com

TIP

Aloha hours, hula dancers, ukulele bands, Sunday luaus, and all Hawaiian beers on tap make Da Kine a refreshing and tempting escape anytime.

JOIN THE NEIGHBORHOOD
AT THE NAGLEE PARK GARAGE

The large picnic tables on the patio of this tiny converted garage declare that when you're at NPG, you're part of the neighborhood. Open only for dinner Tuesday through Saturday and Sunday brunch, this new American eatery with sophisticated comfort food made with local, seasonal ingredients is a beautiful blend of community and outstanding food. A dog- and kid-friendly destination with craft brews on tap makes your visit to the garage a warm and fuzzy one. On selected Wednesdays, May to October, live music including folk, indie, ska, blues, gypsy-ragtime, and jazz is played free of charge. Note that the restaurant's limited seating fills up faster than normal on concert nights, but the local talent is a fantastic value-add to time already well spent.

Naglee Park Garage, 505 E San Carlos St., San Jose, 95112
408-286-1100, www.nagleeparkgarage.com

Good for families

TAKE ON
THE *MAN V. FOOD* TRIFECTA

Remember when *Man v. Food* came to San Jose? Well, yeah. That. For those of you who might have missed it, you can recreate the episode on your own by taking on the *giant* (like, that's an understatement) Burritozilla at Iguanas, trying to survive the Hellfire Challenge (twelve hellfire wingers in ten minutes— no drinks, no napkins) at SmokeEaters, and consuming the massive plate of baby back ribs at Henry's World Famous Hi-Life. Of course, I might also recommend enjoying these places individually and consuming smaller quantities and more than one menu item. But if you find that you ask yourself, "What would food-eating champ Joey Chestnut do?" then this famous food trifecta is something to push to the top of your list.

Henry's World Famous Hi-Life, 301 W St. John St., San Jose, 95110
408-295-5454, www.henryshilife.com

Iguanas, 330 S 3rd St., San Jose, 95112
408-271-9772, www.burritozilla.com

SmokeEaters, 29 S 3rd St., San Jose, 95113
408-293-9976, www.smoke-eaters.com

CELEBRATE OKTOBERFEST
EVERY MONTH AT TESKE'S GERMANIA

A list of things that make a good Oktoberfest: German beer served in giant steins. Insane helpings of sausage and schnitzel. Lederhosen. German hospitality. Really friendly strangers. A polka band that plays German drinking songs followed by Robin Thick, Lady Gaga, Prince, Psy, Johnny Cash, and Frank Sinatra covers. Wait, what was that last one? Oh yes, it's the monthly visit of the Internationals to Teske's! A band—nay, an event—that makes this already genuine Bavarian getaway feel just like Oktoberfest, only with warmer temperatures and more frequently. By the conclusion of the night, you'll be amply satiated with authentic German food, you'll have learned all about German beer, you'll have a million new drinking buddies, and you may want to take the band home with you because they are so adorable. If your cheeks are in need of a smile workout, get down to Teske's and fill up on Deutsche food and frivolity.

Teske's Germania, 255 N 1st St., San Jose, 95113
408-292-0291, www.teskes-germania.com

The Internationals, www.theinternationals.com

SAMPLE TERIYAKI
AND TAIKO AT THE OBON FESTIVAL

July brings to Japantown one of the most anticipated cultural festivals in San Jose (and there are a lot!). Obon is a comparatively intimate festival; however, there is no shortage of food. Gyoza, udon, sushi, tempura, pearl tea, giant vats of boiled corn on the cob, red bean cake called imagawayaki, and seemingly endless grilling pits full of teriyaki are only some of the festival favorites. The signage is clear and the layout of booths is efficient, allowing you less time in line and more eating and taking in the visual feast. Along with the appealing aroma of Japanese cuisine, the powerful boom of taiko (ensemble drumming on large Japanese drums) also fills the air. Seeing San Jose Taiko perform for their own community among the kimonos and festive lantern-lined streets really does make this a feast for all your senses.

San Jose Buddhist Church Betsuin, 640 N 5th St. at Jackson and Taylor
San Jose, 95112, www.sjbetsuin.com/obon/

San Jose Taiko, www.taiko.org

Good for families

SIP AND SURPASS
YOUR GRAPEST EXPECTATIONS

I bet you didn't know that the Santa Clara Valley is California's oldest continuously producing wine region, did you? Well before Napa entered the viniculture arena, this area was producing grapes for the missions. As a result, San Jose offers as many options for sipping fine wine as there are varietals. Copious wine bars, each with its own special mood and focus, can be found all over the city, and Vyne Bistro highlights the option for 3-oz glasses to encourage you to sample more of their expansive local, regional, and international wine menu. The tasting room for J. Lohr Winery is also an option for sampling California's "grapest." In true San Jose spirit, no appointment is needed and no fee is charged for tastings (except for Cuvée Series or limited J. Lohr wines). If you're looking for a winery tour fifteen minutes from downtown San Jose, the historic Testarossa Winery perches in the Los Gatos Hills. With stunning vineyard views, cellar cave tours, a tasting room, and a gorgeous patio shaded by ancient sycamore trees, this is the essence of vini, vidi, vino.

Vyne Bistro
110 Paseo de San Antonio, San Jose, 95112
408-375-2618, www.vynebistrosj.com

J. Lohr San Jose Wine Center
1000 Lenzen Ave., San Jose, 95126
408-918-2160, www.jlohr.com

Testarossa Winery
300 College Ave., Los Gatos, 95030
408-354-6150, www.testarossa.com

CONSUME YOUR WEIGHT
IN PHO AND BAHN MI

As home to the largest Vietnamese population outside of Vietnam, San Jose knows a thing or two about the culinary traditions of this culture. The highly sought-after bahn mi (Vietnamese sandwich) and pho (noodle soup) are more "tame" samples of the cuisine that have been embraced and are enjoyed by pretty much the whole city. While bahn mi shops are almost as common as cafés, Lee's Sandwiches and Dakao are two solid options giving you lots of choices for fillings. For pho, Bun Bo Hue An Nam boasts a stellar reputation backed by "pho-nomenal" taste. For the more adventurous gastronome who is ready to taste first and find out what it was you ate later, an extreme quest awaits you at the Grand Century Mall, which boasts more than two hundred unique Vietnamese shops, including the South Asian food court of your dreams.

Lee's Sandwiches, 260 E Santa Clara St., San Jose, 95113
408-286-8808, www.leesandwiches.com

Dakao, 98 E San Salvador St., San Jose, 95112
408-286-7260, www.dakaosj.wix.com/dakao

Bun Bo Hue An Nam, 740 Story Rd., San Jose, 95112
408-993-1755

Grand Century Mall, 111 Story Rd., San Jose, 95112

Good for families

MANGIA YOUR WAY
THROUGH 1956 AT ORIGINAL JOE'S

Even if you were alive in the '50s or never wondered what it was like, Original Joe's is a perfect and delicious destination. It also happens to be a totally surreal leap back in time. This isn't a kitsch, gimmicky replication 1950s; OJ's is the real deal. A totally authentic Italian '50s eatery run by the same family that opened it in 1956, this iconic restaurant has retained just about all of its vintage flair. Décor, menu, regulars, service; it's a serious wormhole-type trip and a yummy one at that. Joe's Special, veal parmigiana, and a meatball sub grace the gigantic menu, and the plates of pasta are as big as your head. With meals served by waiters in tuxedos and the distinct sound of Italian being spoken in the highly visible kitchen, it's the kind of place where (despite being totally family friendly) you'd expect Tony Soprano to walk in any minute. Or Dean Martin. Or, quite possibly, Marty McFly.

Original Joe's, 301 S 1st St., San Jose, 95113
408-292-7030, www.originaljoes.com

Good for families

JUST CHILL OUT
ON THE PATIO AT THE
SAN PEDRO SQUARE MARKET

Sometimes you need a nice big outdoor space to just chill out. And sometimes you want to bring your dog to that place. Or your kids. Or both. And you don't really want to move more than about one hundred steps all day, which means you need lots of food and drink options in sight. You know, a pizza place, baked potato bar, crepes, fancy/crazy hot dogs, spring rolls, falafel, small-batch ice cream, tacos (obviously), and Venezuelan arepa, something of everything. And then certainly there are times when you want to just chill with beer. Lots of types of beer. Like, lots. And sometimes you'd like this patio of your dreams to have live music, trivia nights, free movie nights, or whiskey tastings. And big screens playing the sports games. Yeah. That. So sometimes you go to the San Pedro Square Market, and you just live the dream, man.

San Pedro Square Market, 87 N San Pedro St., San Jose, 95110
408-817-9435, www.sanpedrosquaremarket.com

Good for families

EAT YOUR BIG,
FAT, GREEK HEART OUT
AT THE SAN JOSE GREEK FESTIVAL

If there were room (and if I had the talent), I'd write an entire Homeric poem about the San Jose Greek Festival. Oh loukoumades, oh gyros, oh baklava, souvlaki, moussaka, and spanakopita, get in my belly. This is a festival that serves up food cooked by local families with recipes passed down for generations. Greek culture is an ancient one, and they have had a few years to perfect things. This *is* your grandmother's melomakarona, and that's a good thing. People have been known to fast the week before, just to make sure they have room for the generous assortment of homemade delicacies. Round out your day (and your stomach) with lively bouzouki and surrounded by award-winning dancers, and you'll leave well versed and ready for next year.

St. Nicholas Greek Orthodox Church, 1260 Davis St.
San Jose, 95126, 408-246-2770, www.saintnicholas.org/greek-festival

Good for families

GET FRESH
AND GO FARM TO TABLE

Before we were Silicon Valley, the region was known as the "Valley of Heart's Delight," and until the 1960s it was the largest fruit production and packing region in the world. For one incredible, delectable night each August, Veggielution, a community farm in East San Jose, holds an astounding dinner they have dubbed Bounty of Heart's Delight. The five-course affair is prepared by a local guest chef using produce from its six-acre garden and orchard, as well as other locally sourced items (including wine and craft beer). The meal, limited to about one hundred very lucky people, is an exclusive farm-to-table extravaganza. You may think you know what fresh is, but definitions will alter as you dine on food from the garden you sit next to. Organic, slow food; this is our wheelhouse. Hayrides and a barn dance round out this bountiful evening.

Veggielution, 647 S King Rd., San Jose, 95116
408-634-3276, www.veggielution.org

Farmers' Markets, www.pcfma.com/markets

Good for families

TIP

You can self-tour the farm any day, and the vegetable stand is open every Saturday if you want to try your own hand at cooking fresh. The city is jam-packed with farmers' markets too, so fresh choices are just as bountiful.

WET YOUR WHISTLE
AT SILICON VALLEY BEER WEEK

While I'm sure many dedicate more than just a week for paying homage to the frosty malt goddess, Silicon Valley makes a special point to revere the fermented beverage deity during Silicon Valley Beer Week. With scores of participating pubs, breweries, microbreweries, and individual beer makers, this event is an educational one, addressing all your burning beer questions. Which beers go with ice cream? What secret ingredient or technique will transform your home brew from meh to marvelous? With an array of beer-food pairings, beer-infused treats, expert panels, and ask-the-brewer opportunities, SVBW is not only an opportunity to discover the craft beer offerings popping up all over, but an insight into the new local movement stemming from a region with such a rich brewing history.

Silicon Valley Beer Week, www.svbeerweek.com

JUST A FEW OF THE LOCAL PUBS AND PARTICIPATING BREWERIES

Original Gravity Public House
66 S 1st St., San Jose, 95113
408-915-2337, www.originalgravitypub.com

Trials Pub
265 N 1st St., San Jose, 95113
408-947-0497, trialspub.com

Clandestine Brewery
1805 Little Orchard St., Suite 124, San Jose, 95125
408-520-0220, www.clandestinebrewing.com

ISO: Beers
75 E Santa Clara St., San Jose, 95113
408-298-2337

O'Flaherty's Irish Pub
25 N San Pedro St., San Jose, 95110
408-947-8007, www.oflahertyspub.com

Strike Brewing
2009 S 10th St., San Jose, 95112
650-714-6983, www.strikebrewingco.com

21 and over only if partaking in alcohol;
please drink responsibly.

Image Credit: Evelyn Soto

ARTS AND ENTERTAINMENT

TELL SUNDAY
YOU AREN'T READY FOR THE WEEKEND TO END AND HEAD TO CAFÉ STRITCH

A balance of casual, hip ambiance (devoid of pretention), well-crafted food, and noticeably absent inflated prices, Café Stritch is a friendly, laid-back, authentically cool space. This seat and serve yourself venue is housed in a large, brick-walled and reclaimed-wood-floored setting, and brings in packed houses for jazz artists who are both big and not-quite-yet-big deals. The vibe is chill and well-behaved, and one of the nicest things about it (aside from their seriously delicious mac and cheese) is the all-ages, diverse crowd that always seems to assemble. The music connects all walks of life and this watering hole, with style and hospitality to spare, feels like home. When Sunday comes, and you aren't ready for the weekend to end, here is where you will find your people.

Café Stritch, 374 S 1st St., San Jose, 95113
408-280-6161, www.cafestritch.com

TIP

Four times a year, Stritch opens on their usually closed Mondays for ShakesBEERience, a fabulously accessible reading of a Shakespeare play that encourages revelry and drinking throughout. Actors interact with the crowd, stand on the bar, and often drink a pint or two along with the audience as they act. This event is very popular and showcases San Jose's outside-the-box/bar/Bard thinking.

"CHALK" IT UP
TO AWESOME AT THE LUNA PARK CHALK ART FESTIVAL

For many, the smell and feel of chalk is extremely nostalgic. Whether used at school or to doodle on driveways growing up, there's something wonderfully innocent and youthful about it. It stays with you and almost beckons you to dream. These same feelings of possibilities and creativity are at the core of the Luna Park Chalk Art Festival, and there is absolutely no limit to the subjects and styles that are represented at this free neighborhood event. Amateurs and professionals alike, side by side, take to the pavement grid to create fleeting, temporary masterpieces! Post-festival chalk sales have been known to spike considerably, as viewing the hundreds of squares has a way of sparking widespread inspiration.

Backesto Park, 651-699 Empire St., San Jose, 95112
www.lunaparkchalkart.org

Good family activity

THINK DEEP THOUGHTS
AT THE SAN JOSE INSTITUTE OF CONTEMPORARY ART (ICA)

I'm the first to admit that sometimes I don't always "get" visual art, especially the more modern pieces; they tend to confuse me. I know I'm not alone. That being said, the opportunity to view conceptually challenging yet visually compelling art is still extremely appealing. If you're in the same boat as I am, drop your anchor at the ICA. They kind of live for compelling and challenging and are there to show you the best of the best in contemporary trends. Perhaps the greatest advantage of the institute (aside from the exhibits) is the fact that it's not a sprawling museum where you feel rushed and overwhelmed. The ICA gives you the time and space you need to reflect on what you are seeing, which, if you're like me, may take a bit of time.

ICA, 560 S 1st St., San Jose, 95113
408-283-8155, www.sjica.org

PUT IT IN PARK
AT THE CAPITOL DRIVE-IN

Raise your hand if you have a better sound system in your car than in your house. Now, keep it up if your car is more comfortable than your living room. That's what I thought. There's a retro charm to a drive-in cinema for sure, but in some cases it's a pretty high-tech way to see a movie. The Capitol Drive-In sets you up with the current blockbusters in all-digital projection, plus double features rain or shine on the cheap, and you can't really beat that. Bring your own food or buy from the concession stand; enjoy from inside your vehicle or tailgate. What's not to like? Okay, you can put your hand down now.

West Wind Capitol 6 Drive-In, 3630 Hillcap Ave., San Jose, 95136
408-226-2251, www.sanjose.org/CapitolDriveIn

Good family activity

GET REEL
AT CINEQUEST FILM FESTIVAL

San Jose has a long history of being first. We're somehow genetically predisposed to early adoption, I think. One of the ways we get to feed our beta-testing sensibilities is the Cinequest Film Festival, one of the finest, friendliest, and most unpretentious film festivals in existence. For over a quarter of a century, Cinequest has been presenting a spectacular lineup of more than two hundred films spanning a two-week period each February and March. They inspire the next generation of filmmakers and their community with independent and foreign film screenings, many of which are world and/or U.S. premieres. They've also been celebrating the mavericks of the industry by hosting conversations with well-known actors, directors, writers, critics, and even technology innovators who develop new kinds of cinematic storytelling. There's a real sense of collective joy when passionate filmgoers sit next to passionate filmmakers, and the power of film is applauded at the conclusion of each screening.

Various locations downtown, www.cinequest.org

TIP
Want to really be first? Buy an Express Pass, which allows you to get your seat before any regular ticket holders do. #Winning.

GO ALL ACCESS
AT THE SAN JOSE JAZZ SUMMER FEST

It would be impossible for me to explain just how big a deal the San Jose Jazz Summer Fest is. Like, thirteen stages impossible. But here's what you need to know. Hands down the best way to experience this massive three-day festival is to go all the way. Get a hotel room well in advance, get plenty of sleep the month before, build up your dance muscles and maybe your alcohol tolerance, and get that VIP all-access pass. Going VIP gives you first priority access to smaller stage events that fill up fast, front of stage access, shaded seating, and unlimited food and drink. This is the way to take in big-name headliners playing the main stage, up-and-coming artists in small club performances, the New Orleans style Big Easy Parade, Jazz Mass, Gospel Brunch, Jazz Jams, swing and salsa lessons, and more.

San Jose Jazz Summer Fest, www.summerfest.sanjosejazz.org
San Jose Jazz, www.sanjosejazz.org

TIP
Can't wait for summer? San Jose Jazz holds a smaller Winter Fest around March and sponsors a number of other one-off music events year-round.

BASK IN THE CLASSICAL GLOW
OF LE PETIT TRIANON

Somewhat hidden off a downtown side street, the beautiful and historic Le Petit Trianon stands noble and proud. Inside the walls of this concert hall, the strum of an acoustic guitar, the delicate notes from a solo harp, and the resounding melodies of a full orchestra warmly fill the entire space. The simple and romantic architectural charm of this miniature palace enhances each resonating chord that's played here. This artistic gem is perfectly suited acoustically for a variety of classical music events, and with a seating capacity of just 350, there isn't a bad seat in the house. Just ask any of the twenty-plus arts groups that make up the Silicon Valley Arts Coalition (South Bay Guitar Society, San Jose Chamber Music Society, the Steinway Society, etc.) if there's a better space in San Jose suited to taking in an orchestra or a solo recital.

Le Petit Trianon, 72 N 5th St., San Jose, 95112
408-995-5400, www.trianontheatre.com

Silicon Valley Arts Coalition, www.svarts.org

RAGE ON DURING ARTRAGE
AT THE SAN JOSE MUSEUM OF ART

The San Jose Museum of Art is undoubtedly a grand excursion anytime, with its gorgeous layout and stunning collections, but one of the most delightful times to visit is during ArtRage. Every two to three months, this after-hours gathering combines your full-access gallery viewing with music, themed activities, shopping, a bit of wine, DIY art activities, lectures, and other cool surprises. It's a fun, eclectic, hip, but by no means necessarily young crowd that attends, and the energy and activities of the night pair well with the current exhibits. ArtRage is a fresh, relaxed, and more immersive approach to the museum for the avid art lover, the newbie, and everyone in between.

San Jose Museum of Art, 110 S Market St., San Jose, 95113
408-271-6840, www.sjmusart.org

EMBRACE A ZANY TRIO
ON A QUIRKY CORNER

What if a crazy donut art gallery, a competitive improv troupe, and an independent film house all shared the same space? I'll tell you what—it would look like 2nd and San Carlos in San Jose. While it might sound like the front for the secret lab of a mad scientist, I can assure you . . . well, actually I can't assure you of anything other than this corner is seriously wacky.

Give your belly a laughing workout with competitive improv at ComedySportz. Combining the best athleticism and fandom of sports (complete with ridiculous ref calls) and spontaneous comedy, this is about as fun as it gets. As "loyal fans" you'll provide the suggestions and the encouragement as two teams battle it out to the hilarious end.

If you find yourself needing a little sugar shock, look no further than Psycho Donuts. Billed as the world's first and only asylum for wayward donuts, they've left no ingredient out in their quest of World Donutization. Pizza, breakfast cereal, foie gras, tequila . . . you name it, they've probably invented a donut with it, and a psycho nurse will serve it to you with a slightly mad grin. Equally inventive local art dons the walls.

The Camera 3 has found its eclectic niche (influenced by its crazy roommates no doubt) with a variety of cult classics, B movies, indie flicks, foreign films, and European productions of operas shown in Sony Digital Cinema 4K and Dolby 5.1 surround sound. Oscar-nominated films and animated shorts fill out this small theater's listings.

ComedySportz, Camera 3, Psycho Donuts
All located at 288 S 2nd St., San Jose, 95113

ComedySportz, 408-985-LAFF, comedysportzsanjose.com

Psycho Donuts, 408-533-1023, www.psycho-donuts.com

Camera 3, 408-998-3300, www.cameracinemas/camera3

Good family activity

MAKE IT A TRIPLE PLAY
AT SAN JOSE STAGE, CITY LIGHTS, AND NORTHSIDE THEATRE COMPANY

Bigger is not always better, and this may never be more true than when it comes to live theater. Theater is, after all, scalable, and sometimes a small theater—one, say, in the ninety-nine-seat range—can connect with you on a level that a larger one (in both seats and budget) may not. San Jose provides a varied performing arts experience with its myriad of intimate, but no less professional, theaters. What these theaters lack in seats they make up for in talent, creativity, technical ingenuity, and in most cases the absence of those annoying body mics. Proximity breeds nuanced, natural movement, the ability to hear a real whisper, and maybe even get a little bit of actor spit on you. San Jose Stage, City Lights, and Northside all provide full seasons of thought-provoking, compelling entertainment with the sweet vantage point of being less than ten rows away from the action.

San Jose Stage Company, 490 S 1st St., San Jose, 95113
408-283-7142, www.thestage.org

City Lights Theater Company, 529 S 2nd St., San Jose, 95112
408-295-4200, www.cltc.org

Northside Theatre Company, 84 E Williams St., San Jose, 95116
408-288-7820, www.northsidetheatre.com

● ●

UNWIND IN STYLE
AT THE HEDLEY CLUB LOUNGE
AT THE HOTEL DE ANZA

From the moment you walk into the Hedley Club, you're taken back to an era of total class and sophistication. An era when a smooth jazz trio was essential to your cocktail lounge experience. The Hedley understands this and pairs its timeless interior with the superior sounds of local jazz artists. Slide on up to the wood-burning fireplace, sip your cocktail by the cherry wood and marble bar, and sneak out to the palm court terrace, all while a swoon-worthy soundtrack scores your movement. The hand-sculpted archways and bass and sax combos seduce in tandem most Wednesdays through Sundays.

Hedley Club Lounge, 233 W San Carlos St., San Jose, 95113
408-286-1000, www.hoteldeanza.com

VISIT THE DRAMATIC PAST
OF FOUR HISTORIC THEATERS ALL INSIDE TWO CITY BLOCKS

It's kind of a crime to lump four gorgeous historic theaters into one must-see, but these sister theaters have been through a lot over the years and are now bonded together by their majestic pasts and blindingly bright futures. These ladies have aged gracefully and proved that age is just a number.

Beyond elegant, the California Theatre is a renovated art deco movie house and now hosts professional opera, symphony, and silent films. Every inch of her is decadent, making her a coveted wedding venue.

The San Jose Center for the Performing Arts (CPA) is the place to be for Broadway touring shows and ballet. The 1972 building was built by the Frank Lloyd Wright Foundation and boasts a plethora of groovy circular architectural elements throughout.

The Rolling Stones, the Who, Morrissey, Frank Sinatra, Barbra Streisand, the Moody Blues, Bob Dylan . . . yeah, they've all played the City National Civic, and after its recent multimillion-dollar renovation, this city landmark is rocking out like she wasn't an octogenarian.

The charming and intimate Montgomery Theater, built in 1936, plays home to Children's Musical Theater (CMT) San Jose, where several stars of Broadway got their start. She may be smaller than her other siblings at 475 seats, but she delivers a powerful theatrical punch.

Information on All Four Theaters
www.sanjosetheaters.org

California Theatre
345 S 1st St., San Jose, 95113

CPA
255 Almaden Blvd., San Jose, 95113

City National Civic
135 W San Carlos, San Jose, 95113

Montgomery Theater
271 S Market, San Jose, 95113

WALK THE WALK
AT SOUTH FIRST FRIDAYS

San Jose's SoFA (South of First Area) District is at the center of San Jose's creative pulse and, through its largely organic, grassroots collaboration, has transformed into its own exciting destination. Since 2005, the first Friday of the month (except January and July) has served as a collective display of the district's unique and ever-evolving arts scene. During the art walk a dozen gallery doors are thrown open until midnight, free to the public. Many have demonstrations, artist receptions, libations, hands-on activities, and other entertainment, but the art doesn't just stay in the places you'd expect. During South First Fridays in particular, you'll find live music and art exhibits at corporate offices and yoga studios too. While a visit to SoFA is always a blast, the art walk is an efficient and immensely satisfying way to experience a ton of art in just a few hours.

South First Friday Art Walk, www.southfirstfridays.com

SubZERO Festival, www.subzerofestival.com

Good family activity

TIP

Each June, South First Friday is taken to a whole new level when they block off the streets, bring in stages, open a beer garden, and welcome blocks of artists' booths. Live body painting, performance art, fashion shows, art cars—anything and everything is possible, and it's a feast they call the SubZERO Festival.

FIND AN AUDIENCE
AT OPEN MIC NIGHT

Move over *American Idol*. Take a number *X Factor*. San Jose is a mecca for budding artists, and pretty much any night of the week you can take in an open mic featuring a parade of potential next big things. From rock and acoustic folk, to opera and classical guitar, and even stand-up comedy, the local and independent coffeehouses are full of opportunities to hear the talent of tomorrow over delicious coffee. And if the spirit moves you, sign up and show 'em what you've got.

Philz Coffee, 118 Paseo de San Antonio, San Jose, 95112
408-971-4212, www.philzcoffee.com

Caffé Frascati, 315 S 1st St., San Jose, 95113
408-287-0400, www.caffefrascati.com

Lift Café, 5883 Eden Park Place, San Jose, 95138
www.cafeliftsj.com

SKIP THE WAITING
AT MUSIC TUNNEL KTV CAFE

What's the worst thing about karaoke? It has to be waiting for you or your friend's turn to come around, right? Music Tunnel totally fixed that by providing private karaoke rooms that can accommodate anywhere from three to twenty-five people. Take your pick from over 120,000 songs, including selections in many different languages, and a room where you are the boss. There's a strict no alcohol and no-smoking policy enforced here, so it's a perfect place for mixed-age groups and lots of milk teas. The full menu has an Asian flair to it and the sound systems are state of the art. Take control of your karaoke experience with this popular retreat.

Music Tunnel KTV Café, 1132 S De Anza Blvd., San Jose, 95129
408-446-0888, www.musictunnelktv.com

Good family activity

GET DOWN
WITH THE DOWNTOWN PUBLIC ART WALK

Just a quick stroll around downtown and it's easy to see why San Jose was ranked one of America's Top ArtPlaces in 2013. From the airport and the convention center to city hall and San Jose State University, there are hundreds of amazing public art installations. Over the years we've seen the Downtown Doors program and the Art Box Project SJ transform utility doors and utility boxes with art by local high school students and professional artists. Murals, phantom galleries that appear in the windows of unleased office space, and even interactive art make it impossible to go a single block without running into urban masterpieces. Grab a map or explore organically.

Downtown Public Art Walk, www.sanjose.org/PublicArt

Phantom Galleries, www.phantomgalleries.com

Eco-City Cycles, 408-771-7723, www.ecocitycycles.com

Good family activity

TIP

If you want to cover more ground, one of the best ways to see the city and its art is to hire an Eco-City Cycles pedicab (for two) and take in the art and the open air with an amiable cycle guide! It's safe, fun, and a green way to get about, plus you can negotiate your fee up front for custom trips!

HAVE YOUR VISION ADJUSTED
BY TEATRO VISIÓN

What is perhaps most significant about Teatro Visión is that they describe their productions as a service to the community. This Chicano theater company is deeply invested in telling stories and entertaining its audience, but also in nurturing the next generation of community leaders and cultural ambassadors in their audience. Checking their egos at the door and harnessing the arts to inspire a better civic family, this group excels at presenting a phenomenal blend of specifically Chicano and Latino narratives that are also universally engaging and powerful. Many of them are performed partly or entirely in Spanish with supertitles, but even if you don't speak a word of Spanish, the talent and production values are so high caliber that they easily transcend any perceived language barrier. As an added bonus, most of the performances are held at the School of Arts and Culture at Mexican Heritage Plaza, a stunning modern facility with tremendous presence and technical capability.

Teatro Visión, 408-294-6621, www.teatrovision.org

School of Arts & Culture at Mexican Heritage Plaza,
700 Alum Rock Ave., San Jose, 95116
408-794-6250, www.schoolofartsandculture.org

BECOME AN ART COLLECTOR
FOR $2 A POP AT KALEID GALLERY

Think art collecting is only for the wealthy? Think again. Luckily, you don't need to be making a Silicon Valley sized income to become a certified buyer and patron, thanks to the Kaleid Gallery and its beyond awesome $2 Tuesdays. Rock up to their sixty-plus-member art co-op and explore sculpture, collage, painting, jewelry, photographs, and art from just about every medium. Smaller works, sketches, and prints by the artists are set at just $2 for this monthly event, which often has demonstrations, activities, or performances scheduled too. You see, sometimes it *is* the little things that count.

Kaleid Gallery, 88 S 4th St., San Jose, 95113
408-271-5151, www.kaleidgallery.com

Good family activity

MAKE AN ARTS DISCOVERY
AT THE THEATRE ON SAN PEDRO SQUARE (TOSPS)

On the second floor of the historic Farmers Union Building, surrounded by exposed wood beams and century-old brick, sits a theater with approximately 150 of the most comfortable, wide, leather seats with perfect views of the stage. On that stage a full season is produced by the resident (and also managing) Tabard Theatre Company. When Tabard isn't performing new works, musicals, and family-appropriate theater, that stage, known as the Theatre on San Pedro Square, hosts a free Tuesday-night music series, comedy, film, dance, and many other events befitting "the destination for arts discovery in Silicon Valley." To the left of the TOSPS stage is a really huge and gorgeous bar. All together, the TOSPS is the kind of space that may inspire a feeling of love at first sight. With its great atmosphere and diverse lineup most nights of the week, it's a tough act to follow.

TOSPS, 29 N San Pedro St., San Jose, 95110
408-679-2330, www.tabardtheatre.org

Good family activity

IMMERSE YOURSELF
IN EAST INDIAN DANCE WITH THE ABHINAYA DANCE COMPANY

Classical South Indian dance is alive and thriving in San Jose. This complex art of depicting Hindu and Indian mythology through precise movement (and live musical accompaniment) is one with an ancient tradition and a strong future. Total commitment to comprehensive training is required as this is an exact art requiring intense physical discipline over many years to perfect. This dance genre enlists the help of the whole body, even the eyes, to flawlessly communicate layered, complex stories. Students start young and work diligently toward being awarded a solo performance (arangetram), and any opportunity to catch a community event or student debut is an uncommonly experienced wonder to behold.

Abhinaya Dance Company, 408-871-5959, www.abhinaya.org

EXPECT THE UNCOMMON
WITH THE COMMONS

Beatbox cello? A performance from a poet laureate? A progressive full orchestra flash mob? Interpretive ballet? A violinist/acrobat who plays upside down? Anything is possible with the Commons. There's no box you can put this artistic entity in. They defy description and would reject your label on principle anyway, but this somewhat underground group is dedicated to supporting artists and holding a combination of planned and spontaneous art events around town. Be it park or warehouse, this group performs sporadically and randomly, but if you can catch them, I'm confident you will leave saying, "Well, you don't see that every day." The odds are in your favor you may not have ever seen it before, or ever again.

The Commons, www.thecommonssj.com

Good family activity

ROCK YOUR SOCKS OFF
AT THE ROCKBAR THEATER

Grab your leather jacket, studded belt, leopard print, and your party animal, because the RockBar Theater is going to make you feel like you've been pulled from the back of a line, past the red velvet rope, and handed a VIP all-access pass. With hardcore rock décor, skulls, candles, and plenty of throne-like seating, this place feels like something out of *MTV Cribs* and will school you in rock star lifestyle a few hours at a time. A distinctive music palace with live punk, indie, metal, '80s pop, and classic rock shows on the docket, you can expect both tribute bands and the real deal. This bastion of rock and roll preserves the in-your-face days of music, courtesy of the fifty-foot stage. Also, a great thing about this haunt: the vodka bar, featuring a hundred types of vodka, allowing you to rock the rocktail, head bang, and fist pump your way through the night.

RockBar Theater, 360 Saratoga Ave., San Jose, 95133
408-241-3150, www.rockbartheater.com

SPORTS

TRY NOT TO DROOL ALL OVER THE SHOWROOM
AT THE SILICON VALLEY INTERNATIONAL CAR SHOW

The cars of tomorrow, the newest models, concept cars, gadgets for your favorite means of personal transportation, collectibles—it's all there in shiny amazingness at the Silicon Valley International Car Show. I'm just going to need to ask those prone to excitable salivary episodes to please bring your ShamWow with you to avoid any embarrassing puddles. Pulling in huge crowds and an unbelievable list of vendors in a massive exhibit space, there's nothing small or understated about this show. It's the sexy beast of car shows to be sure. I repeat, for the safety of yourself and others, please see to your own spittle.

San Jose McEnery Convention Center
150 W San Carlos St., San Jose, 95113
www.svautoshow.com

Good family activity

JAM WITH THE SILICON VALLEY
ROLLER GIRLS

Flat track roller derby—it's just as exciting and empowering and fierce as you think it is, and it's happening in San Jose. The KillaBytes, Dot.Kamikazes, and the Hard Drivers are the league's A, B, and C teams, and these ladies . . . who am I kidding, they aren't ladies, not on the track they aren't. These women will blow you away with their speed and skill. If you haven't had a chance to see a bout before, there's nothing to worry about. It's easy to follow and the diehards who are most likely sitting near you will be happy to fill you in on the rules. Complete with fun names, colorful commentary, and the best uniforms of any sport, this is a special club with a cult following and shouldn't be missed.

Silicon Valley Roller Girls, www.svrollergirls.com

Good family activity

SENSE SERIOUS SEISMIC ACTIVITY
WITH THE SAN JOSE EARTHQUAKES

Call it soccer or football or footie, but any way you label it, the Quakes fans are rabid and the team is A+, making for an all-around brilliant time when you attend a home game. Combine the team's talent with Avaya Stadium's natural grass field, its gorgeous open air, and sustainable solar roof assets, and you really are living by California rules. The stadium also happens to be, in true geek city fashion, the first cloud-enabled professional sports stadium using next-generation tech to deliver the most engaging digital fan experience. Oh, and did I mention the new stadium has the largest outdoor bar in North America? The 3,647-square-foot slab supports 45 beers on tap. Just thought I'd mention that. So what are you waiting for? Follow the Ultras' lead and chant along, "Goonies never say die!"

Avaya Stadium, 1123 Coleman Ave., San Jose, 95110
408-556-7700, www.sjearthquakes.com

Good family activity

DIVE HEAD FIRST
INTO THE SHARK TANK

While you might initially laugh at the idea of a city with such a warm climate having an NHL hockey team, San Jose bleeds teal for their Sharks and you will too. With a rapscallion mascot (SJ Sharkie) who repels from the arena rafters and TP's visiting team fans (several of our home game traditions involve the Jaws theme), we might have the most fun of any fans. Plus, we have the loudest fans in the league, and volume has to count for something, right? The Sharks consistently make it to the playoffs and are a class act organization on and off the ice. They may not have the number of Stanley Cups representative of their skill and fan loyalty (yet), but one home game and you'll see why the SAP Center is called the Shark Tank, even when it's hosting world famous music acts.

SAP Center at San Jose, 525 W Santa Clara St., San Jose, 95113
408-999-5757, www.sharks.nhl.com

Good family activity

GET YOUR MOTOR RUNNIN'
AT HOT SAN JOSE NIGHTS

Gearheads get hoppin' when July rolls around, because that means it's time for hot rods, muscle cars, aircraft, food, music, and just a good ole time at Hot San Jose Nights. Collectors come out of the woodwork each year to display their vintage, restored beauties and talk a bit of shop. This is a super popular event with kids, and chairs and coolers are essential as there's a lot of ground to cover. Car people are some of the coolest, nicest folks around, and this event showcases not only some amazing machines but some of the most skilled and genuinely sweet, splendidly passionate people.

Reid-Hillview Airport, 2500 Cunningham Ave., San Jose, 95148
408-929-2256, www.hotsanjosenights.com

Good family activity

BAT A THOUSAND
WITH THE SAN JOSE GIANTS

A World Series ticket can be hard to come by, not to mention budget busting, but a chance to see championship players before they make it to the majors is a short, affordable walk. With an impressive team record and unusually accessible and friendly players, a San Jose Giants home game showcases the best of San Jose's no-ego, down-home vibe. Tim Lincecum, Buster Posey, Matt Cain, and Madison Bumgarner, to name a few, are all SJ Giants alums, and many kids have the autographs (signed before every game) to prove it. The stadium has you very close to the action and opts to forgo digital ads for fun traditions like the beer batter (when the designated "beer batter" from the opposing team strikes out, beer becomes half price!). A home run outing for kids and fans, a game is even a winner among the baseball apathetic.

Municipal Stadium, 588 E Alma Ave., San Jose, 95112
408-297-1435, www.sjgiants.com

Good family activity

TIP
Postgame fireworks are scheduled for special nights throughout the season, usually announced in March, adding an additional element of oooh and aaahhh.

FLIP FOR THE TALENT
AT LAKE CUNNINGHAM REGIONAL SKATE PARK

If you want to see gravity being inexplicably defied, roll on over to Lake Cunningham Regional Skate Park. At sixty-eight thousand square feet, LCRSP is the largest skate park in California. Featuring the world's largest cradle, tallest vert wall, largest full pipe, plus a totally rad variety of terrain for all skill levels, it's kind of like Leonardo DiCaprio in *Titanic*. You know, "I'm the king of the world!" If the park could talk, I'm pretty sure that's what it would say. Watching boarders and bladers pivot and biff is not for the weak of heart, mind you, but it is exhilarating. If you aren't already a Tony Hawk in training, a visit to this place may be the gateway that gets you hooked. Four-wheeled participants *might* want to make note of the nearest hospital, just in case a landing decides to nail you.

Lake Cunningham Regional Skate Park, 2305 S White Rd., San Jose, 95101
408-793-5510, www.sanjose.org/SkatePark

Good family activity

SCORE A TOUR
OF LEVI'S STADIUM

Levi's Stadium set the bar very high as a standout stadium experience. So high it's host of Super Bowl 50. Yes, the 49ers scored big time with the smartest and greenest stadium in the NFL. Even if you don't get to see a game here, the tour is a pleasure for both the football fan and the geek. Should you fall into the overlapping section of that Venn diagram, you may need to pace yourself so you don't overheat. Tours of Levi's give the uber-fan an unprecedented, behind-the-scenes look at all the tech and innovation that you'd expect from the Silicon Valley. There's a whole lot of awesome here. Combine your guided tour of the stadium with the twenty-thousand-square-foot 49ers Museum and explore the eleven galleries and exhibit spaces housing, among other things, five glorious Lombardi Super Bowl championship trophies.

Levi's Stadium, 4900 Marie P. Debartolo Way, Santa Clara, 95054,
415-464-9377, www.levisstadium.com
Light Rail, www.vta.org

Good family activity

TIP
There's a light rail stop right at the stadium, a cheap and easy way to get to and from the stadium.

SEE THE NEXT X GAMES CHAMP
TUCK A NO HANDER AT CALABAZAS BMX PARK

A beautiful park of its own accord, Calabazas also happens to have the largest city-funded BMX course of its kind in the Bay Area, with few rivals in the rest of California. Bring your bikes if you count yourself among the dexterous and revel in the extremeness of it all. For those of you who feel a tad misclassified as land mammals and have put coordination on your birthday wish list more than a few years, there are benches on which you can channel your powers of extreme spectating. Mad bike skills seem to grow like weeds out here, and most days you can find groups of brave athletes practicing their moves in this sweetest of spots.

Calabazas Park, Rainbow Drive and Blaney Ave., San Jose, 95129
www.sanjose.org/BMX

Good family activity

CULTURE AND HISTORY

HONOR THOSE WHO SERVED
AT THE VETERANS DAY PARADE

You will be hard-pressed to find a more moving event than the San Jose Veterans Day Parade presented each year by the United Veterans Council of Santa Clara County in partnership with the city. Since 1919, an opportunity to see and hear first-hand the sacrifices made by our service men and women has been provided in the form of this parade. It is a ceremony with floats, music, marching, military vehicles, and plenty of celebration, but it also carries with it a lot of heart, honor, history, pride, and pain, so bring your tissues and your gratitude. The stories told and the guests who share at the memorial ceremony preceding the commencement of the parade will leave an indelible mark.

Veterans Day Parade, Downtown San Jose, www.uvcscc.org

Good family activity

STOMP GRAPES
AT LITTLE ITALY'S
ITALIAN FAMILY FESTA

For a weekend you can be part of one big familia! Join dreamy tenors, the Fratello Marionettes, and the entire Italian community at the Italian Family Festa held each August in Little Italy. Play bocce ball, partake at the wine garden, delight in culinary demonstrations, join in traditional folk dancing (oh, you *will* be asked to join in at some point, you can count on it), and prepare yourself for . . . So. Much. Food. Taking the prize for one of the most anticipated events of the entire festa is the Grape Stomp. Dress up in your best Lucille Ball digs (or not) and get your feet wet in an actual barrel of grapes. This contest sees teams of two (one stomping and one keeping the juices flowing into the jug) competing for the title of "Brava Squadra D'Uva."

Italian Family Festa, 408-293-7122, www.italianfamilyfestasj.org

Little Italy, W Julian and N Almaden Blvd., San Jose, 95110
www.littleitalysj.com

Good family activity

DISCOVER
ONE OF THE LAST THREE REMAINING
JAPANTOWNS IN THE UNITED STATES

San Jose's bustling Japantown artfully fuses its long history and beautiful heritage with a tight, active community, creating a colorful city district popular with both locals and tourists. Authentic Japanese restaurants, art galleries, a year-round farmers market, and specialty shopping thrive here, and stores that have been in operation for over one hundred years are fixed right next to the newest hangouts. Stores selling traditional bonsai, Japanese string instruments, and kimonos, interspersed with an organic dog treat shop, premier sneaker consignment store, and a tattoo parlor make this an outstanding place to spend the day exploring. You never know what to expect here, except of course a great time.

Japantown, near 5th and Jackson, San Jose, 95112, www.jtown.org

Japanese American Museum, 535 N 5th St., San Jose, 95112
408-294-3138, www.jamsj.org

Good family activity

TIP
For a really moving experience, take a tour of the Japanese American Museum led by internment camp survivors.

· ·

WALK LIKE AN EGYPTIAN
AT THE ROSICRUCIAN MUSEUM

Indiana Jones and Laura Croft have nothing on you, because you have the Rosicrucian on your side and the Rosicrucian is home to the largest collection of Egyptian artifacts in western North America. With four thousand artifacts, a replica tomb, a planetarium, and an alchemy garden, you're in for an education fit for a pharaoh. This is no pyramid scheme; even the museum itself was modeled after the Temple of Amon at Karnak. Special lectures and kids' activities are scheduled a few times during the day, so check the schedule first thing so you don't miss anything you might want to participate in.

Rosicrucian Museum, 1660 Park Ave., San Jose, 95191
408-947-3635, www.egyptianmuseum.org

Good family activity

TIP

Kids seventeen and under need
to be accompanied by an adult
at least eighteen years of age
at all times.

MARVEL AT THE MAJESTY
OF THE CATHEDRAL BASILICA
OF ST. JOSEPH

The Cathedral Basilica of St. Joseph has taken a licking and kept on ticking, suffering earthquake damage, fires, and a total of five iterations previous to 1885. Made a minor basilica by Pope John Paul II in 1997 in recognition of its beauty, history, and service, this beloved city landmark is one of perseverance and splendor. If you think the exterior is magnificent, just wait until you step inside and discover the exceptional craftsmanship of its thirty-nine stained glass windows, some of which were created in Germany with mouth-blown Bavarian glass made from a formula dating back to the eleventh century. An ornate altar and painted frieze add to the grandeur of the cathedral as do the spellbinding acoustics. If you can catch one of many public concerts held there, it's an unforgettable feeling.

Cathedral Basilica of St. Joseph, 80 S Market St., San Jose, 95113
408-283-8100, www.stjosephcathedral.org

GO ADOBE TO ADOBE
WITH WALKS AND TALKS

One of the city's best resources is San Jose State University, and one of the most educational and fun ways for a visitor (or resident) to get a feel for San Jose's layout and legacies is with a Walks and Talks tour. Keen young SJSU students lead you on a professional, structured, but light and fun tour lasting about an hour. From the Peralta Adobe (San Jose's first historic landmark) to technology giant Adobe's headquarters, this tour illuminates the innovative spirit that drove the pioneers here hundreds of years ago and is still so present in the city. The synergy of the old and new (given by the next generation of citizens) will have you smiling as will some of the historical accounts and rarely divulged city secrets.

Walks and Talks start and end locations depend on the tour.
www.sanjosewalksandtalks.org

LIVE IN THE PAST
AT HISTORY PARK AT KELLEY PARK

At the south end of Kelley Park sits a charming mix of twenty-seven original and reproduction homes. Many of the buildings house small museums including the Chinese American Historical Museum at the Ng Shing Gung, the Portuguese Historical Museum at the Impario, the African American Heritage House at Zanker House, and the Museum of the Boat People and Republic of Vietnam at the Greenwalk House. A blacksmith shop, old gas station, stables, a print shop, and even an ice cream parlor (best malts ever) make up fourteen acres of the most fabulous Throwback Thursday you ever saw. Far enough from road sounds, History Park really does take you back to the early 1900s. Tours (given on weekdays) are very informative and there are plenty of places to picnic and soak up a bit of the past.

Entrance located at 635 Phelan Ave., San Jose, 95112
www.historysanjose.org/wp/plan-your-visit/history-park

Good family activity

FALL IN LOVE
WITH THE MUSICAL HEART OF MEXICO AT VIVAFEST

A celebration of the vibrant Mexican heritage and the art of mariachi cannot possibly be limited to a single day or even a weekend. Therefore, VivaFest, which happens to be just such a celebration, occurs over more than a month. The passion, music, and people that make up VivaFest defy the boundaries that contain other cultural festivals, spreading the majority of the celebration through September and October. Pueblo numero uno (as San Jose was originally called) pulls out all the stops for this colorful and amazing cultural extravaganza that features concerts, master classes, mariachi, plenty of food, art, speakers, and community conversations that happen almost everywhere in the city.

Multiple locations, www.vivafest.org

Good family activity

GET IN THE SPIRIT
AT WILLOW GLEN'S ROSE, WHITE & BLUE PARADE

For a town of a million, San Jose still has lot of small-town qualities and simpler time feels. One endearing display of these types of unaffected sensibilities is the annual Rose, White & Blue Parade, which takes place on the Fourth of July in the Willow Glen neighborhood. In a fun throwback to days gone by, you can watch streamer-decorated wagons carrying costumed pets, vintage autos, horses, floats, local school marching bands—all the things you'd expect from a tiny town parade. Okay, so there might be a few iPads snapping photos as the parade passes by, and grand marshals have included Steve Wozniak, but aside from that you'd think you were miles away from the capital of Silicon Valley. Stick around for the picnic, car show, dancing, live music, and artists' booths.

Rose, White & Blue Parade, www.rosewhiteblueparade.com

Good family activity

GET IN THE RIGHT STATE OF "MINE"
AT ALMADEN QUICKSILVER COUNTY PARK & MINING MUSEUM

An old mercury mine and a museum honoring its past might seem about as fun as touring Chernobyl at first, but once you put away your fear of blood poisoning or falling down a deserted mine shaft, this outing will likely make its way up to the top of your list. The part mining played in San Jose's history, the immigrant labor and its economic impact, is all well documented at the museum and is really a fascinating account many locals don't even know about. It's a niche excursion for sure, but between exploring the vast scenery of the park and the museum itself, it's an easy full day of historical hiking.

Almaden Quicksilver County Park & Mining Museum
21350 Almaden Rd., San Jose, 95120
408-323-1107, www.newalmaden.org/AQSPark

Good family activity

SHOPPING AND FASHION

GET ADDICTED
TO LIFE ON THE ROW AT SANTANA ROW

Attention, shopping zealots! Santana Row, the city's undisputed premiere shopping destination, is calling you. Pick up already! With its comfortable blend of high-end, accessible, and niche stores, plus several salons and spas to cater to your exhausted, post-shopping-marathon bodies, it's not just recreation—it's a way of life. The indoor and sidewalk dining options are chic and plentiful, providing an array of stops for refueling, relaxing, and for showing off your new purchases. This boutique, balconied paradise, reminiscent of European fashion districts, is beautiful in and of itself, only adding to the likelihood that you may never want to leave. If that's the case, if another day (or two) is in order, no problem: the centrally located Hotel Valencia can accommodate those who still have some credit cards needing love.

Santana Row, 377 Santana Row, San Jose, 95128
408-551-4611, www.santanarow.com

TREASURE HUNT
ON SAN JOSE'S ANTIQUES ROW

Part museum, part shopping, and all awesome, San Jose is an antique junkie's paradise. Even the casual hobbyist and the newbie antique-curious will have a field day walking San Jose's Antiques Row. Dozens of stores along West San Carlos Street, spanning several blocks, are each packed to the gills with a history told in knickknacks, hat racks, lamps, books, pots, jewelry, clothes, furniture, and probably the idol from the first Indiana Jones movie. Whether you're looking for something specific or just looking, start at the Antiques Colony, a collection of fifty quality dealers in a nine-thousand-square-foot showroom and the largest antique collective in Silicon Valley. It is the anchor store for the rest of the row and will help steer you in the right direction based on your wants or needs. Take your time looking, and if you happen to find that perfect thing or things, prepare to negotiate!

The Antiques Colony, 1881 W San Carlos St., San Jose, 95128
408-293-9844, www.antiquescolony.com/allaboutus

Rose Garden Vintage and More, 1883 W San Carlos St.
San Jose, 95128, 408-286-6631

Briarwood Antiques & Collectibles, 1885 W San Carlos St.
San Jose, 95128, 408-292-1720

Burbank Antiques, 1893 W San Carlos St., San Jose, 95128, 408-292-3204

GET ALL SPRUCED UP!

Gentlemen, when was the last time you had a proper, luxurious, professional shave? One with the really incredible hot lather and a straight razor? With a little splash of cologne and talc at the end? Don't pretend to be all "whatever"—we all know you like a bit of pampering just as much as the ladies. Crewners knows. And what's more, they'll fix you right up with that shave. And if you want to lower your ears while you are at it, you're in luck: they'll set you up with a stylish cut too. The price of two bits has gone up a bit since proper barbershops were commonplace, but you're worth it.

Now, girls, I wouldn't forget you. Are you ready to coax your inner bombshell out of hiding? Ready to be a little daring? A little retro? Studio Glam has three remarkable stylists who can enhance what you've got with a cut, color, style, makeup, or any combination thereof. However, their specialty is quite special. Take your new look to that timeless pinup era and get a photo shoot to boot. Your very own private pinup party, courtesy of Studio Glam, pairs your pin curls and ruby lips with a classic car, vintage clothing, and a sassy pose. Preserve the day you coerced your innermost moxie out into the open with photos.

Crewners (at the San Pedro Square Market), 87 N San Pedro Ave. San Jose, 95110, 408-663-1813, www.crewners.com

Studio Glam, 311 Stockton Ave., San Jose, 95126 408-260-5001, www.studioglam.com

VISIT VINYL PARADISE

You don't have to miss the days of flipping through records, admiring the cover art, nor do you have to miss listening to that nonreplicable sound of a needle on vinyl. True, the musical trip down memory lane is less and less accessible in general these days, but San Jose holds on to its old and showcases it alongside all our shiny new. The city is a proud leader of the resurrection of vinyl popularity, which sees small local businesses supporting other small businesses. More and more, bars and restaurants are fixing up their record players and are choosing vinyl over streaming. Vintage vinyl DJ nights are increasingly popular too, and Streetlight Records and Needle to the Groove are two of the go-to places for hard-to-find, rare, mint condition records. Rediscover this lost art from the center of the movement taking place at these shops. They'll spin you right round baby, right round.

Streetlight Records, 980 S Bascom Ave., San Jose, 95128
1-888-330-7776, www.streetlightrecords.com

Needle to the Groove, 410 E Santa Clara St., San Jose, 95113
408-418-3151, www.discogs.com/seller/needletothegroove

ANSWER THE CALL
OF YOUR INNER INTERNATIONAL
FASHIONISTA AT THE AO DAI FESTIVAL

A lavish display unlike any other, the annual Ao Dai Festival is, in a word, gorgeous. A celebration of Vietnamese art and culture, fashion (the Ao Dai is the long gown and pants traditionally worn by women in Vietnam) is at the center of this event, and it is absolutely stunning. Designers from Vietnam as well as the region are tasked with promoting the grace and beauty of Vietnamese women, and the results and artistic display of the fashion are just exquisite. Silks flow, golden threads glow, and grace is exhibited from head to toe each May. You'll be hard-pressed to find a more elegant and unique fashion event in the Bay Area.

Ao Dai Festival, www.aodaifestival.com

TIP

While the main fashion show is a paid event (with proceeds going to help orphans in Vietnam), you can catch one hundred models, along with stilt walkers, music, and a dragon dance for free, preceding the gala.

SCRATCH THAT SHOPPING ITCH
AT THE SAN JOSE FLEA MARKET

Vintage bicycle parts? Sure. A couch you swear was in your grandmother's house? Probably. Every kind of produce known to man? Definitely. The glowing briefcase from *Pulp Fiction*? I'm not going to say no. You can pretty much find any item you desire at what remains the largest open-air flea market in America. It might take you a bit to get through the 120 acres of booths selling everything from palm trees to perfumes, but if you can walk it, you can probably find it. This family tradition since 1960 may even have unsold items from the first day the market opened! You might even stumble across R2D2 or the treasure of Sierra Madre! Make sure you charge your cell phone before entering the flea, just in case you get lost.

San Jose Flea Market, 1590 Berryessa Rd., San Jose, 95133
408-453-1110, www.sjfm.com

Good family activity

PARKS AND RECREATION

GET CONNECTED TO NATURE
THROUGH PLAY AT HAPPY HOLLOW PARK AND ZOO

With its puppet theater and its kiddie rides, this Association of Zoos and Aquariums–accredited zoo is a visual feast for children, but the extraordinarily up-close viewing of rare animals appeals to the youngster in all of us. This intimate zoo has a collection of highly threatened and endangered species exhibited with great care and employing incredible ingenuity to provide the visitor optimal vantage points for observation and education. Around each corner is a surprise in the form of lemurs, giant anteaters, or capybara. Happy Hollow was also the first zoo and amusement park to be LEED Gold certified, so it's fun to see the park's solar power, water runoff collection systems, and vegetated roofs at play as you explore this locally adored icon.

Happy Hollow Park and Zoo, 1300 Senter Rd., San Jose, 95112
408-794-6400, www.hhpz.org

Good family activity

TIP

Honey from the Happy Hollow beehive is harvested by the local 4-H club and beekeeping class members. The honey is then sold in the gift shop with all proceeds going to support mountain gorillas in Virunga National Park, one of the zoo's global conservation partners. Pick some up in the store for a sweet deal!

Image Credit: Evelyn Soto

STOP AND SMELL THE ROSES
AT THE MUNICIPAL AND HERITAGE ROSE GARDENS

There are those in the "every rose has its thorn" camp, and then there are those who know anytime you can place yourself in the middle of thousands of rose bushes, it's a pretty awesome day. The Heritage Rose Garden and Municipal Rose Garden are colorful and unexpected floral gems that thrive in San Jose's urban setting. Acres and literally thousands of blooms burst with color and fill the air with fragrance at these two gardens of paradise.

Heritage Rose Garden, Spring and Taylor Sts., San Jose, 95110
www.heritageroses.us

Municipal Rose Garden, Naglee Ave. and Dana Ave.
San Jose, 95126, 408-794-7275, www.sanjose.org/MRoseGarden

Good family activity

GET FIT TO A TEE TIME
AT CINNABAR HILLS GOLF CLUB

A game of golf can be made or broken by the course, the company, and the weather. While I can't do a thing about the company you keep, I will point out that San Jose's weather is sunny, on average, three hundred days a year. Combine that fact with the picturesque, quintessentially California view from the Cinnabar Hills Golf Club, plus its champion-caliber courses, and you have a pretty good chance of achieving two out of three. Choose between the club's three nine-hole courses—the Canyon, the Lake, or the Mountain. Even the nongolfer—you know, the one you dragged along—will be wooed by the lush hilly views, wild turkeys, hawks, and even deer. From sunrise to sunset, this magical place is one you can easily relish. I'd bet my nine-iron on it.

Cinnabar Hills Golf Club, 23600 McKean Rd., San Jose, 95141
408-323-7814, www.cinnabarhills.com

FIND YOUR ZEN
AT THE JAPANESE FRIENDSHIP GARDEN

San Jose's first of seven sister cities, Okayama, Japan (established in 1957), was just the third sister city affiliation in the United States after the inception of the national program in 1956. Rain or shine the Japanese Friendship Garden, modeled after the famous Korakuen Garden in Okayama, is serene, totally Zen, and downright pretty. Wander the six-acre garden and marvel at its three koi ponds complete with wild egrets landing and wading among them. The very model of tranquility, this is a lovely place to be at one with your thoughts on all of San Jose's awesomeness.

Japanese Friendship Garden, Senter Rd. and East Alma Ave.
San Jose, 95112, 408-794-7275, www.sanjose.org/JFG

Good family activity

CONQUER THE LONGEST LEG
OF THE COYOTE CREEK TRAIL

The Coyote Creek Trail is one of the longest trail systems, extending from the bay to San Jose's southern boundary and beyond. The southern reach goes from Tully Road to Morgan Hill, near Anderson County Park, and measures 16.8 miles. While not terribly difficult with regard to climb, it is a good distance, and making the thirty-three-mile round-trip certainly earns you a big dinner. It's a challenge on bike and even more so on foot, but you'll see all manner of transportation taking on this popular trail. Also visible as you glide down the paved path are pastoral views of waterways, rural and urban settings, copious flora and fauna, and ospreys as you approach Morgan Hill.

Coyote Creek Trail, www.sanjose.org/CoyoteCreekTrail

RIDE THE GIANT CONCRETE SLIDES
AT BRIGADOON PARK

Life is short, and sometimes the greatest joys, the most memorable moments, are those with their foundation in silly, simple, childish whims. There are 193 parks in San Jose, each with its own perks and personalities, and Brigadoon Park is no exception. Carved into the sides of the park's hill are massive concrete slides. When perched upon a piece of cardboard (which often can be found at the base of the slide, left for community use), you can reach some remarkable speeds. It's a slide. It's not a lap in a NASCAR race car, and it's a bit of a trek to the top, but it's a fun little exercise in glee generation that is free, simple, and guaranteed to put a smile on your face.

Brigadoon Park, Brigadoon Way and Maloney Drive, San Jose, 95121
www.sanjose.org/brigadoon

Good family activity

SCARE YOURSELF SILLY
WITH A FLASHLIGHT TOUR OF THE WINCHESTER MYSTERY HOUSE, IF YOU DARE

It's only one of the most famous and most haunted houses in the world. But you can handle all the stories of documented paranormal activity surrounding the home of Sarah Winchester, heir to the Winchester rifle fortune. You're not the least bit scared to walk the halls of this massive (and quite beautiful) home. I can tell, when you walk up a staircase that just stops, you aren't going to lose it. And I'm sure you won't have a problem when you come to doors that open to brick walls. Now, how about if you did all of that at night, with the house lights out and only a flashlight to guide you? And what if it were Friday the 13th? Or Halloween night? Changes the whole setup now, doesn't it? Well, what's the holdup? Chicken?

Winchester Mystery House, 525 S Winchester Blvd., San Jose, 95128
408-247-2101, www.winchestermysteryhouse.com

Good family activity

TIP

The winter holidays see the house and grounds decked out with lights and Victorian-style decorated trees, bringing out an entirely different kind of spirit. And don't let the fame of the house force you to overlook the gardens. The grounds are immaculately kept, and it's worth a look especially if you are botanically inclined.

CELEBRATE THE HOLIDAYS
SAN JOSE STYLE

It's just a three-hour drive from San Jose to a snow lover's paradise, but real San Jose natives bask in the glow of a mild and even sunny winter full of ice skating under palm trees, nostalgic animatronic holiday displays, and carnival rides. From November to early January, downtown smells like warm churros, fresh kettle corn, and evergreens. The city knows how to close out a calendar year.

Downtown Ice, Circle of Palms, 127 S Market St., San Jose, 95113
www.sjdowntown.com/downtownice

Christmas in the Park, 101 West Santa Clara St., San Jose, 95113
408-200-3800, www.christmasinthepark.com

Winter Wonderland, www.winterwonderlandsj.com

Good family activity

The Downtown Ice rink at the Circle of Palms is not only an incredible opportunity to skate without a coat, but a feat of engineering befitting our metropolis. Built each year for two months of skating, the LED light displays on the palms are programmed to the music playing while you skate.

Across from the ice rink, Christmas in the Park takes over all of Cesar Chavez Park. With music (both live and piped-in holiday classics), hundreds of small trees decorated by community groups, moving displays, a stage for local performers, and lights, lights, and more lights, it's as festive a place as you'll ever find and chock-full of families taking it all in.

Winter Wonderland is adjacent to Christmas in the Park and dots the nearby paseos and parts of the park with an assortment of carnival rides. Open late, some of the rides give you a stunning bird's-eye view of all the lights and stars at night.

INDULGE
IN THE ULTIMATE ROYAL TREATMENT AT THE DOLCE HAYES MANSION

A lavish hotel plus an extravagant on-site spa equals an escape any movie star would crave; but courtesy of the Dolce Hayes Mansion, it's all made totally accessible to those who are only celebrities in their heads. Six miles south of downtown, this lush historical estate with fantastic mountain views awaits you even if your name isn't Brangelina. You've been good, I know you have, so it's only right that you treat yourself to some real R & R. Some world-class rest in this grand hotel and a few spa indulgences from the endless list of decadent treatments will whisk your stress clean out of the atmosphere. Plan on at least two full days and nights here for optimal benefit.

Dolce Hayes Mansion, 200 Edenvale Ave., San Jose, 95136
866-981-3300, www.hayesmansion.com

GET COCKY
AT EMMA PRUSCH FARM REGIONAL PARK

Upon parking at Emma Prusch Farm, you'll be greeted by chickens. And these chickens, along with an inordinate number of roosters, will very likely seduce you with their extensive range of clucks and chortles. As you make your way toward the grass and barn, you'll realize there are scores of the most ridiculously beautiful chickens you have ever seen roaming free without a care in the world. And you will likely have never seen so many different kinds of chickens in your life. Every color, shape, and size, all getting along great, making you want to *be* a chicken. Can't we all just be chickens? Then you will see a dozen or so peacocks just walking around in the open, perching in trees and on fences and picnic tables. You might conclude you've died and arrived at your eternal reward. It's that wonderful. Stay for the kite flying, 4-H happenings, and the historic orchard, but come for the exemplary roosters and peacocks.

Emma Prusch Farm Regional Park, 647 S King Rd., San Jose, 95116
408-794-6262, www.sanjose.org/EmmaPrusch

Good family activity

WITNESS A WHOLE LOT OF DOGS
HAVING THEIR DAY AT BARK IN THE PARK

Unleash your inner hound and sniff out the ultimate treat for doggie devotees. Each September, Bark in the Park provides a variety of canine competitions, copious belly rubs, and some prime slobbering opportunities. I'm not going to lie, there's also quite a bit of butt sniffing among the four-legged attendees. This is a no judgment event, however, so it's all good at this gathering of pooches and their people. Don't have a dog? No worries. That just translates into more free hands for petting and throwing Frisbees! Tail wagging, costume, and owner/dog look-alike contests are just a few of the events you can look forward to at this all-day festival. Added bonus? All proceeds benefit the Campus Community Association and local pet charities.

Bark in the Park, William Street Park, William and South 16th Sts.
San Jose, 95112, www.barksanjose.org

Good family activity

GO SEASONAL
AT ALUM ROCK PARK

It's been said that San Jose doesn't have any real seasons, and while our awesome weather is relatively constant, there are lovely ways to experience the gentle California transitions much more dramatically. Alum Rock Park, the first municipal park in California, is one of these places. This wild and rustic park with thirteen miles of trails is set on 720 acres. With the east/west and south sides of the park on opposite sides of a canyon, the two halves see a whole different set of flora and fauna, making it possible to see major changes from one week to the next. Various wildflowers in spring, flowing creeks and striking green hills in the winter, golden brown grasses in the summer, and foliage change in autumn make this a park for all seasons.

Alum Rock Park, 15350 Penitencia Creek Rd., San Jose, 95127
408-794-7275, www.sanjose.org/AlumRock

Good family activity

BRAVE BOMBS AWAY
AT RAGING WATERS

Take your average waterslide. Now pump it full of energy drinks and have John McEnroe give it a pep talk. Now step into an enclosed capsule, wait for the floor to drop out from beneath your feet, and proceed to plummet through an enclosed, inverted looping flume for over two hundred feet. Now you have Bombs Away, perhaps the most exhilarating of the attractions at the twenty-three-acre Raging Waters. It's pretty intense and not for the faint of heart. Good thing there are plenty of less amped-up slides available for the more passive water enthusiast. Adrenaline junkies and traditional waders alike can appreciate the calming Endless River, which allows you to float throughout the park in an inner tube for hours.

Raging Waters, 2333 S White Rd., San Jose, 95148
408-238-9900, www.ragingwaters.com

Good family activity

TIP
Rent a private cabana in advance
for the ultimate in shaded personal
space, which is hard to come by
on the park's busiest days.

GIDDYUP
AT GARROD FARMS AND COOPER-GARROD ESTATE VINEYARDS

What better way to get into the spirit of the West than on a horse? Garrod Farms, in the hills of neighboring Saratoga, provides some superb views of San Jose during the hour-long trail rides. Rides can be arranged as early as 8:30 a.m., seven days a week, and all levels of riders can be accommodated. For extra fun do the ninety-minute trail ride first thing Saturday or Sunday morning (8:30 a.m.) or the wine tasting ride, which occurs on the last Sunday of the month and includes wine tasting after your ride at the historic 120-acre Cooper-Garrod Estate Vineyard. Inside the tasting room, aviation aficionados will want to see the photo exhibit of George Cooper's career as a NASA test pilot. Additionally, you can take an extensive tour with the winemakers on certain days, an ecotour/hike through the vineyard's ecosystem, or just tour the facilities on your own.

Garrod Farms, 22647 Garrod Rd., Saratoga, 95070
408-867-9527, www.garrodfarms.com

Cooper-Garrod Estate Vineyards, 22645 Garrod Rd., Saratoga, 95070
877-923-4616, www.cgv.com

FIND YOUR INNER CHILD
AT THE CHILDREN'S DISCOVERY MUSEUM

It's no wonder we have more baby geniuses per capita than anywhere else in the world. Okay, maybe that's not a totally accurate statistic, but when Steve Wozniak invests in a museum for kids, you better believe it's going to be one that will wow and entertain as well as educate. It also might be where tech companies recruit their future engineers or where your child (or a legitimately borrowed child) discovers his or her own interests and talents. The museum caters expertly to all age groups (even under one) and to all the senses. Fostering curiosity and a love for lifelong learning is at the core of each of the exhibits in this 52,000-square-foot cultural pearl, so be prepared to come back again and again and again.

Children's Discovery Museum, 180 Woz Way, San Jose, 95110
408-298-5437, www.cdm.org

Good family activity

SOAR ON FLIGHT DECK
AT CALIFORNIA'S GREAT AMERICA

If aliens ever visited earth and saw amusement parks, I'm certain they'd wonder what we'd all done to deserve to be strapped into such hideous torture contraptions. What crime warrants being spun about until we puke, or left dangling upside down until we nearly pass out from screaming? Surely we couldn't be voluntarily subjecting ourselves to such horrifying g-forces, not to mention the sunburn and the sugar crashes? And yet we're an odd little bunch of humans and Great America is proof. There are dozens of amazing rides at this thrill-seekers' paradise, but Flight Deck achieves a ridiculously first-class effect. Reaching speeds of fifty mph while suspended below the track, feet left dangling free, you loop on the outside of the track, take on two 270-degree afterburn turns, engage in a zero-gravity roll, and navigate a huge full circle wingover, mere feet from water. Sorry aliens, some of us just like these kinds of things.

California's Great America, 4701 Great America Pky., Santa Clara, 95054
408-988-1776, www.cagreatamerica.com

Good family activity

TIP

The very front of this ride
is worth the extra wait at least
once, as the view is one hundred
percent unobstructed by seats in
front of you, leaving your exact
path more of an unknown and
adding an extra rush.

MIND THE GEEK

GET YOUR GEEK ON
AT THE TECH MUSEUM OF INNOVATION

An exemplary model of geeky awesomeness, the Tech Museum has an interactive appeal that has kids and adults of all ages making their techy pilgrimages over and over. Interactive exhibits on genetics, space, music, biology, geology, and more, amaze and educate while simultaneously telling a uniquely San Jose/ Silicon Valley story. So much of the technology at the center of scientific breakthroughs has come from this valley, but the technology used to exhibit these narratives is also in many cases born right here. Be sure to get to the earthquake simulator, the space jet pack chair, and don't miss catching an educational film shown on the truly astounding and immersive IMAX.

Tech Museum, 201 S Market St., San Jose, 95113
408-294-8324, www.thetech.org

Good family activity

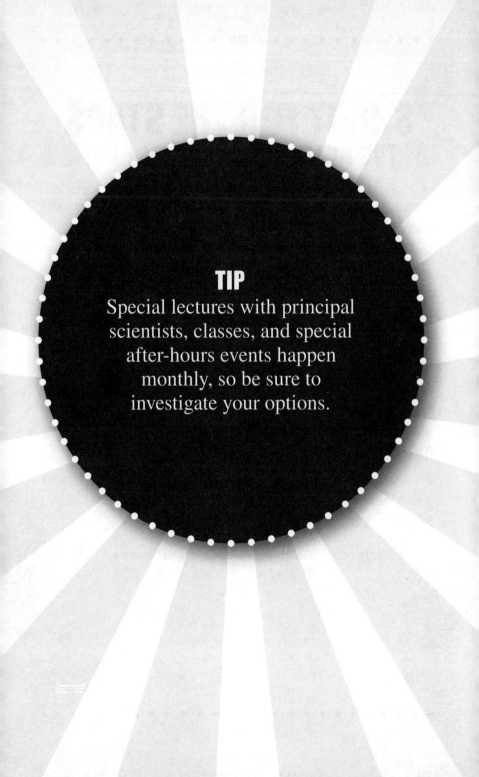

TIP

Special lectures with principal scientists, classes, and special after-hours events happen monthly, so be sure to investigate your options.

SHOOT FOR THE STARS
AT LICK OBSERVATORY

Forget for a moment that planets have been discovered with the telescopes at Lick Observatory and just imagine what it took James Lick to build it. Maybe even cooler than viewing celestial bodies millions of light-years away from atop Mount Hamilton is the mind-blowing story of how a true visionary made it so. For starters, constructing a road up 4,209 feet of mountain in the 1870s was no walk in the park. Navigating observatory materials (including huge telescope lenses shipped from Germany) through 365 turns, by horse—also not easy. Any chance to visit this place is liable to blow your mind, but if you're visiting over a weekend in June to August and can get tickets, the Music of the Spheres series is by far the best "big bang" for your buck. A lecture by a leading scientist, two telescope viewings/tours, and a music concert all in one makes for a long, long night, but one that is truly out of this world.

Lick Observatory, 7281 Mt. Hamilton Rd, Mt. Hamilton, 95140
408-274-5061, www.ucolick.org

TIP

If you need to break up the drive, the strategically placed and aptly named Grand View Restaurant is about halfway up. Surf and turf paired with a stunning view of the sunset can make for an auspicious overture to your night of stargazing.

TOUR
THE GUADALUPE RIVER PARK LIKE A TRUE GEEK: BY SEGWAY

When in Rome, as they say, and when in San Jose, travel geek style because local Steve Wozniak would want it that way. Besides feeling like you are the CEO of a startup during the dot-com boom while upon your trusty mechanical steed, the Segway is an easy and fun way to explore a large area for those who don't need to live the weekend warrior lifestyle. With minimal effort you can soak up some sun, view tons of local wildlife, and learn a bit about the city. Tours start at the Tech Museum (perfect for before or after a visit to the museum or the IMAX) and fill a couple of hours beautifully.

Guadalupe River Park Trail, www.grpg.org/river-park-gardens

Silicon Segway, 650-355-8655, www.siliconsegway.com

Good family activity

POWER UP
WITH INDIE MUSIC AND RETRO VIDEO GAMES AT ROCKAGE SAN JOSE

It's been debated in certain circles whether some of San Jose's festivals may have come into being as the result of a dare. An innocent competition to come up with the oddest or most awesome combination of things to join may very well have been the catalyst for Rockage. For three days in February, the city celebrates the unlikely but epic marriage of indie music and retro video games. Like a geeky play on wine pairing, attendees can couple forty-plus indie bands with arcade free play of Centipede, Super Mario Brothers, Pac-Man, Zelda, Q*bert, and many, many more. As a product of geek stamina prowess that is so evident in San Jose, arcade machines have been known to overheat and start smoking during the festival. Adding to the music and gaming madness are panels, tournaments, and prizes. Oh, and it's all streamed live, obviously. You're welcome.

Various locations, 408-924-6350, www.rockagesj.tumblr.com

Good family activity

GET ANIMATED
AT FANIMECON

Have you heard of the Japanese style of animation called anime? Did you know there's also a huge convention called FanimeCon, celebrating the tradition of anime, manga, and related arts and culture? Did you know it's been held for over twenty years in San Jose? Did you know that it attracts more than twenty thousand fans every year? Did you know that the cosplay is totally off the hook at the event? Did you also know that the city of San Jose officially declared May 23 Fanime Day in honor of the event, which takes over all of downtown and beyond. Well, now you know. Only thing left to do is go experience it for yourself.

San Jose McEnery Convention Center, 150 West San Carlos
San Jose, 95113, www.fanime.com

Good family activity

SPIN YOUR WHEELS
WITH SAN JOSE BIKE PARTY

Every month, delightfully madcap bike enthusiasts take to the streets for the San Jose Bike Party. Themed rides like Monsters vs. Aliens, Steampunk, and Mardi Gras see creatively costumed cyclists parading down city streets, music playing and lights flashing as they go. Themes are announced early on the website along with a playlist to get you pumped up, but actual routes remain secret until twenty-four hours before the party. Designated safety bikers called "birds" keep everyone safe, helping with directions and making sure rules of the road/ride are respected. The "ravens" cycle with large garbage cans in tow, dedicated to making sure no trash (feathers, streamers, food, etc.) is left behind. During the ride, participants flock en masse to a designated space where music, food trucks, and socializing commence. Combining imagination and eco-friendly transport, this all-ages event is a fine example of the typical, inclusive fun San Jose is teeming with.

Various locations, www.sjbikeparty.org

Good family activity

CHECK OUT
ONE OF THE COOLEST LIBRARIES EVER

Standing 136 feet tall with a footprint of over 475,000 square feet and containing 1.6 million volumes, the Dr. Martin Luther King Jr. Library is like the Andre the Giant of libraries. With eight floors full of quiet corners, views of the city, special collections, and even a telescope for viewing the city hall peregrine falcons, this joint venture between San Jose State University and the San Jose Public Library System is a sight to behold. From the giant digital book return tally as you enter, to the Ira F. Brilliant Center for Beethoven Studies and the Martha Heasley Cox Center for Steinbeck Studies, it's a learning space I bet literacy champion LeVar Burton would wholeheartedly endorse. Free one-hour tours of this glorious house of reading can be arranged ahead of time and occasionally can be accommodated on a drop-in basis.

Dr. Martin Luther King Jr. Library, 150 E San Fernando St.
San Jose, 95112, 408-808-2000, www.sjlibrary.org

FLOCK TO SEE
THE CITY HALL PEREGRINE FALCONS

Move over Kardashians! Clara and Fernando El Cohete, the city hall peregrine falcons, have reached celebrity status few people, let alone birds, ever obtain. These two are part of an incredible survival story that saw the species recently come back from the brink of extinction, and as a result they have gathered quite the collection of fanbirds. The aviary soap opera unfolds eighteen stories above ground, and like any good reality show the lens of a remotely operated camera transmits their every move. Highlights include courtship, mating, eggs arriving, hatching, banding day, and the nerve-wracking fledging. The city is entranced February through June, with voter turnout never higher than when falcon baby name suggestions from local elementary school students are on the ballot. Fanbirds can be seen racing about in May, hoping for a glimpse of a successful first flight or, in the case of a fledgling fail, the opportunity to protect any fallen baby until a qualified scientist can inspect and transport it back to safety.

Nest Box, 200 E Santa Clara St., San Jose, 95113
408-535-4800, www.sanjose.org/falcons

Good family activity

PASS GO
AND COLLECT $200 ON THE WORLD'S LARGEST MONOPOLY BOARD

If only there were a way to take one's love for board games and combine them with one's love of physical activity. If only there were a place where one could roll gigantic dice outside. If *only* there were a giant, record-breaking Monopoly board complete with all the houses, properties, and get-out-of-jail cards that I could rent and play with my friends in the sun. I mean, I'd trade Marvin Gardens to have the opportunity to run about wearing a helmet with the Scottie dog Monopoly piece on it. Wait? You mean I can? There is? Wow! I feel like I just won second prize in a beauty contest!

Monopoly in the Park, 180 Woz Way, San Jose, 95110
www.monopolyinthepark.com

Good family activity

FIGHT THE GOOD FIGHT
DURING THE FEATHERS OF FURY PILLOW FIGHT

It's a pretty amazing world we live in, where we can take some of our pent-up, fast-paced, digital stress and release it by smacking the holy living tar out of someone, in public, with a fully sanctioned, official pillow fight. It happens once a year in February, and the exact downtown location is only revealed twenty-four to thirty-six hours in advance. Why? Oh, we don't know, it's just more fun that way. And geekier because you have to keep checking Twitter or Facebook to get the details. Oh wait, we kind of do that already. Getting into the fray is fun and safe and totally family friendly. The feathers fly while some people try to curl up and sleep in the middle, and then everyone lends a hand cleaning up the feathers. Good times and sweet dreams.

Downtown San Jose, www.pillowfightsj.blogspot.com

Good family activity

STAND AT THE INTERSECTION OF ART
AND TECHNOLOGY AT THE ZERO1 GARAGE

When it comes to geeky art, the Zero1 Garage takes it into overdrive with its rotating exhibits. This very accessible gallery, rustic like an art loft but packed with wicked futuristic bits and pieces, features cutting-edge art with its foundation in science. You can feed your poet and your geek simultaneously on installations that include elements of video, augmented reality, sensory lighting, data analysis, real-time interaction, biology, chemistry, DNA, and 3-D printing. The small space employs friendly attendants who'll put you at ease if you aren't sure what you are looking at; plus, with plenty of opportunities to meet the artists, you can feel like you're adding IQ points with each visit. Performance art, lectures, the works happen here, and the electronic artistic expression is one very specific to Silicon Valley.

Zero1 Garage, 439 S 1st St., San Jose, 95113

408-606-6800, www.zero1.org

GET ON BOARD
AT THE EDWARD PETERMAN MUSEUM
OF RAILROAD HISTORY

Trains hold a special place in our not-so-very-distant past, and with a bullet train in the works, they remain a key part of our future. The introduction of the train in San Jose made hundreds of new things possible and thrust the region into an era of economic prosperity. The Edward Peterman Museum of Railroad History, a free museum run by the South Bay Historical Railroad Society, is appropriately located on the Union Pacific Santa Clara freight yard in full view of freight and passenger trains coming and going. The museum includes a smorgasbord of railroad artifacts, detailed history, and railroad maps from the 1860s, but the real gems of this museum are the two full-scale model railroad displays. Get on board.

South Bay Historical Railroad Society, 1005 Railroad Ave.
Santa Clara, 95050, 408-243-3969, www.sbhrs.org

Good family activity

TIP
Live bluegrass every second Sunday at the
Santa Clara Depot? Yes.

SUGGESTED ITINERARIES

BROS AND BREWS

FAMILY FUN

FOOD ADVENTURER

• •

OUTDOOR EXPLORER

THEATER GEEK

ACTIVITIES
BY MONTH

JANUARY

Silicon Valley International Car Show, 63

FEBRUARY

Cinequest, 39

Feathers of Fury Pillow Fight, 131

Rockage San Jose, 125

San Jose Jazz Winter Fest, 41

MARCH

Cinequest, 39

San Jose Jazz Winter Fest, 41

APRIL

Municipal and Heritage Rose Gardens Peak Seasons, 99

MAY

Ao Dai Festival, 92

City Hall Falcon Fledge Watch, 129

FanimeCon, 126

Municipal and Heritage Rose Gardens Peak Seasons, 99

• •

OCTOBER

NOVEMBER

DECEMBER

INDEX

• •

• •

• •

● ●

• •